◆◆◆◆◆◆◆◆◆◆◆◆◆◆◆◆

Captain
Cook

◆◆◆◆◆◆◆◆◆◆◆◆◆◆◆◆

Captain Cook

BY
JON NOONAN

ILLUSTRATED BY YOSHI MIYAKE

CRESTWOOD HOUSE
NEW YORK

Maxwell Macmillan Canada
Toronto

Maxwell Macmillan International
New York Oxford Singapore Sydney

To my favorite teachers, especially Gregory Benford, Herminia Cadenas, Carl Christol, Robert Deckard, Barbara MacEachern, George Saito and Shirley Schaefer.

Copyright © 1993 by Crestwood House, Macmillan Publishing Company
CRESTWOOD HOUSE
Macmillan Publishing Company
866 Third Avenue, New York, NY 10022

Maxwell Macmillan Canada, Inc.
1200 Eglinton Avenue East, Suite 200
Don Mills, Ontario M3C 3N1

Macmillan Publishing Company is part of the
Maxwell Communication Group of Companies

First Edition
Book design by Sylvia Frezzolini
Printed in the United States of America

10 9 8 7 6 5 4 3 2 1

LIBRARY OF CONGRESS CATALOGING-IN-PUBLICATION DATA
Noonan, Jon.
Captain Cook / by Jon Noonan. — 1st ed.
p.   cm — (The Explorers)
Includes Index.
Summary: Discusses the life and travels of the eighteenth-century British navigator and explorer known for his adventurous voyages and maps of the Pacific.
ISBN 0-89686-709-9
1. Cook, James, 1728–1779—Juvenile literature. 2. Explorers—Great Britain—Biography—Juvenile literature. [1. Cook, James, 1728–1779. 2. Explorers.] I. Title. II. Series: Noonan, Jon. Explorers.
G246.C7N66   1993   92-8231
910′.92—dc20
[B]

CONTENTS

◆ ◆ ◆ ◆ ◆ ◆ ◆ ◆ ◆ ◆ ◆ ◆ ◆

COOK AND CREW CROSS THE EQUATOR

From high overhead, the excited teenage boy fell from the sky. Carried on a strip of wood attached to a slipping rope, the lad landed in the ocean off the side of the sailing ship. *Splash!* His fellow shipmates laughed and cheered. As the ship moved, the waves splashed into the boy's face until the rope was pulled up by his shipmates.

The sailing ship, the *Endeavour* (en-'dev-or), was commanded by Lt. James Cook. In future voyages he would be called Captain Cook. Cook was leading his crew across the Atlantic Ocean. Having left England two months earlier, they were crossing the **equator** on October 25, 1768.

Cook let the crew follow the tradition set in earlier times. Those men crossing the equator for the first time were given a choice. They could go for a ride in the ocean or give up four days' worth of rum. The teenage crew members got the first choice only. In all, at least 20 sailors chose the ocean. One by one, they took their turn.

A long rope was guided through a wood block attached at one end of the longest **crossbar** of the main **mast.** The sailor was tied to a strip of wood that went between his legs. A second piece of wood was attached for him to hold in his hands and a third strip was tied above his head.

Then some of his shipmates pulled on the rope. The ocean-choosing sailor was lifted up in the sky to the crossbar. The wood strip above him saved him from getting clobbered at the top. At a signal, the shipmates let go and the sailor fell freely into the ocean. He was hoisted (pulled up) again two more times before his turn was completed.

It was Cook's first time across the equator too. Commanders did not like their crews to dunk them in the sea. Cook chose to give up the rum when his turn came. Cook was glad to let his crew have some fun, as long as they didn't slow the voyage. His main concern was his important **expedition** for science and exploration. He and the scientists on board were going to observe Venus as it moved across the face of the Sun. Cook was

also sent to search for the legendary Southern Continent, said to be in the South Pacific.

How did Cook get chosen as the commander of such a voyage? From his childhood, one might think he would have been likely to become a farmer.

YOUNG JAMES COOK

Cook as a Boy

James Cook was born on October 27, 1728, in Marton, a small village among the farmlands of northeastern England, near the towns of Ayton and Great Ayton. His Scottish father, James Cook, Sr., worked as a laborer for farm owners.

The Cook family lived in a tiny two-room clay cottage. James grew up with his brother John, who was born one year earlier. Several other children were born after James, but only Margaret and Christiana lived past the age of five. Deaths from childhood diseases were still common at that time.

When James was seven years old, his father went to work at a nearby farm called Airy Holme.

The owner, Thomas Scottowe of Great Ayton, saw that James's father had good farming skills. He made him the farm manager in charge of all the crops, supplies, animal care and other farm work.

The Cook family moved into a sturdy house made of stone. Thomas Scottowe sent James to an Ayton school and took care of the costs. James was given lessons in arithmetic, reading and writing by his teacher, Mr. Pullen.

The Challenge of Sailing Ships

As he became a teenager, James learned he could choose a career other than farming. At age 16 he went to work as a clerk for William Sanderson, a friend of Thomas Scottowe's, at his store in the town of Staithes, about 15 miles away.

Staithes stood on the shore of the great North Sea. Looking out from Sanderson's shop, the ocean seemed to spread to the ends of the earth.

Beyond the town's fishing boats, large sailing ships often came into view. These ships always sailed across the coast. Staithes was too small a stop for them. They continued on to England's larger shipping centers.

As the weeks went on, Cook considered the challenge of sailing ships. Sailing seemed like an exciting way to live.

After a year and a half of service in the store, Sanderson could see that James strongly wished to change from a clerk to a sailor. He went with Cook to Whitby, about ten miles to the south, to meet shipowner, John Walker.

The Beginner

Most lads began their sailing careers at ages 11 to 15. Almost 18, James was a bit old to be a beginner at sea. Yet Sanderson saw something special in Cook, and Walker soon recognized it too. Walker accepted him as a trainee. Cook was a quick learner. Like his father, he showed skill in his work.

Walker's ships sailed along the English North Sea coast carrying coal to London. They were bigger than the small fishing boats Cook saw in Staithes. The first ship Cook sailed on, the *Freelove,* was 106 feet long and 27 feet wide. The second one, the *Three Brothers,* was even larger. Both ships were built in Whitby. In these ships, James Cook learned his first lessons on how to sail large ships across the sea.

Cook Gets to Sail

Some lessons were not easy to master. Sand banks, sunken shelves of rock, and storms along unmarked and unlighted coastlines made sailing in the North Sea challenging. At one end of the voyage lay the ship-crowded Thames (temz) River in London. At the other, hundreds of the same ships elbowed for space at Shields on the Tyne River, near the Newcastle coal mines in northern England.

When on land, Cook lived at Walker's house in Whitby, where he often studied **navigation, mathematics** and **astronomy.** Besides the wind, ocean current, sails and rudder, a top sailor made use of mathematics and astronomy for steering the ship. The ship's instruments and the positions of the Moon, Sun, other stars, planets, Earth and the ocean floor were used to guide the ship correctly.

NEW SAILING CHALLENGES

At age 20, in less than half the time of most trainees, Cook was made a full seaman. Then he looked for new challenges. On his very next ship, he sailed across the North Sea to Norway. Within a few years, Cook also sailed the ocean to the Netherlands, the Irish Sea and the English Channel.

In 1755 Walker offered Cook the command of one of his ships, the *Friendship*. Like the first ships he had sailed on, the *Friendship* would be used in the coal trade along the eastern English coast.

Cook was still looking for new adventures. Although Walker was giving him a great honor in trusting his ship to his former trainee, Cook chose to take another course. He joined the Royal Navy.

An Uncommon Choice

Cook's choice was not a common one. At that time, few sailors entered the navy of their own free will. Deadly diseases like **scurvy** awaited those who stayed long at sea. The navy was also known for its poor food, cramped shelter, low pay, hard work and cruel punishments.

The ships were much larger than the coal-trade ships, but they were also much more crowded. They carried lots of extra men to replace the large numbers that often died from disease, icy storms or battles.

Cook soon showed success even under these conditions. With his sailing skills well learned, he moved up swiftly through the titles of the seaman's class. After the first month of naval service, Cook was advanced from an able seaman to a master's mate. A few months later he became the boatswain, in charge of the ship's boats, sails and other gear.

For almost two years Cook served the navy in the ocean waters between England and France. The Seven Years' War between the two countries had just begun. They fought over the control of lands in Canada and America.

In 1757 Cook was given the higher rank of master. He was soon sent to Canada. The navy ships carried soldiers to fight the French there.

In Canada Cook became known as a top sailor and chart maker. He showed that he could guide ships safely through narrow channels and along rocky coastlines. He charted much of the south-eastern coasts of Canada.

In October 1762 Cook came home to England. That December he found time to marry Elizabeth Batts, age 21.

For the next five years, through the spring, summer and early fall, Cook returned to Canada to explore and chart its eastern coasts. For this important task he was given command of his own ship, the *Grenville*. Each autumn Cook sailed home to England to see his family during the winter.

In November 1763 Cook came back to England and saw his first child, James, then seven weeks old. Cook bought his family a home close to London in a village called Mile End Old Town. In the years ahead, the Cooks would have six children.

Cook the Scientist

One summer, Cook showed extra skill as an astronomer. On August 5, 1766, the Moon passed in front of the Sun, causing an eclipse to be visible from Newfoundland in Canada. Cook was charting its coast at the time. Using telescopic tools,

Cook measured the time and progress of the eclipse.

Compared with measurements made at the same time in England, the numbers Cook recorded were used to tell the **longitude** of Newfoundland. In Cook's time, finding the longitude of locations was still a new science. Without knowing the longitude, sailors might sail for hundreds or thousands of miles along a **latitude** line until they found the place they were seeking.

Cook sent his findings to the Royal Society, a group of important scientists in England. They appreciated Cook's effort.

In June 1769 the planet Venus would be traveling across the face of the Sun. The Royal Society asked the Royal Navy to provide a ship to go to the southern Pacific Ocean to observe this event.

The Royal Navy also wanted a ship to go to the same ocean to find a new continent to claim for England. The two goals could be handled on the same journey. The Royal Navy agreed to the voyage. When the Royal Navy chose a commander, they decided upon James Cook. The admirals had taken note of Cook's excellent sailing, charting, scientific and leadership skills.

THE *ENDEAVOUR*

Cook was given command of the sailing ship *Endeavour,* a Whitby-built ship like the ones Cook had sailed before he joined the navy.

To arrive in time to observe the Venus event, the ship sailed from England in August 1768. The *Endeavour* carried Cook, 71 officers and sailors, 12 marines, 4 scientists, 2 artists and 4 servants. Among the scientists was Charles Green, who studied stars and planets, and Joseph Banks, who studied plants and animals.

After crossing the equator, Cook came to the coast of Brazil in November. After getting fresh supplies, Cook continued on to the southern tip of South America. Bypassing the Strait of Magellan

to save time, Cook sailed around stormy Cape Horn and entered the Pacific Ocean.

After crossing Cape Horn in January 1769, Cook and the *Endeavour* crew sighted no islands during February and March.

Three months at sea was enough time for signs of scurvy to show. Yet Cook's crew stayed free of this disease caused by lack of vitamin C. Cook was one of the first commanders to insist that his crew eat vegetables and drink fruit juices to keep themselves healthy during the voyage.

Scurvy took the lives of many sailors of earlier voyages. It usually set limits to exploration, especially in the wide Pacific Ocean. Because of the crew's diet, however, Cook was able to sail as far as he wished.

On to Tahiti

Thanks to Cook's sailing skills and knowledge of latitude and longitude, the *Endeavour* landed at the island of Tahiti on April 13, seven weeks ahead of the Venus crossing.

In those days Tahiti was one of the few islands in the Pacific whose location was known, thanks to the visit of the English explorer Samuel Wallis two years earlier.

Covered with tropical trees and mountains, Tahiti was 33 miles long. Its tallest peak rose over

7,000 feet above sea level. It was a land of small animals, bananas, yams, coconuts, breadfruit, and tall, strong native islanders.

Before the *Endeavour's* landing boats went ashore, Cook gave some commands. His most important rule was that the natives be treated with kindness and fairness.

Then Cook and some of the scientists and crew stepped on the shore. At first, the islanders seemed shy. Then a chief came forward and gave Cook's group a leaflike branch from a banana tree. Everyone gathered one branch each. Hundreds of the natives then walked with Cook, the sailors and the scientists into the breadfruit and coconut groves of the island.

About a half mile inland, the Tahitian islanders cleared the ground of plants. Then everyone laid the leafy branches on top of the cleared area. "Thus peace was concluded," wrote the scientist Joseph Banks.

Over time, feasts of fish, coconut milk, breadfruit and other island foods were given. The islanders showed friendship easily and much trading took place.

After several weeks, Cook and his crew came to know the Tahitians. They were very clean people. They washed themselves three times a day and rinsed their mouths with water after every

meal. They liked to play games and have fun.

They also liked to steal things, however. There was evidence that they also killed some of their own people in ceremonies. At times, they fought wars with other islanders.

To be careful, Cook built a strong fort around an observation area at the northern tip of the island. He called the outpost Fort Venus.

Fort Venus

The scientists did not want to miss this crossing, or transit, of Venus. It would happen on June 3, 1769, and last only six hours. The event would not occur again until the years 1874 and 1882, and then also in 2004 and 2012.

On June 1 and 2, Cook had his officers set up two more observation areas with tents, telescopes and clocks, one to the west and the other to the east of Fort Venus. By the evening of June 2, everything was ready.

Then June 3 arrived. "This day proved as favorable to our purpose as we could wish," Cook wrote. "Not a cloud was to be seen the whole day, and the air was perfectly clear, so that we had every advantage we could desire in observing the whole of the passage of the planet Venus over the Sun's disk."

The Southern Continent

Cook had now completed the first of his two missions. The crossing of Venus had been observed and recorded. His second mission was to seek the great Southern Continent.

For centuries, explorers and **geographers** felt certain that a giant continent, as large as Europe and Asia combined, would be found in the South Pacific. They thought it had to be there to balance the earth.

Before reaching Tahiti, Cook had sailed the *Endeavour* farther south than anyone before him. After leaving Tahiti in August 1769, he searched the southern waters again.

No sign of the Southern Continent was seen. Then the youngest member of Cook's crew, 12-year-old Nicholas Young, sighted New Zealand. Cook named the first landmark "Young Nick's Head" in Nicholas's honor.

Cannibals

After Cook and some of his crew took landing boats to the shore, the New Zealand islanders, the Maoris, came to see them.

Tupia, a native of Tahiti, had come along on Cook's voyage. The Tahitians and the Maoris spoke the same Polynesian language. After listening to the New Zealand natives for a while,

Tupia said to Cook, "These men are not our friends."

The Maoris were cannibals. They killed and ate people as food.

Still, Cook tried to make friends with them anyway. He was kind to their children and gave them gifts. The cannibals did not eat friends. In the future, Cook would bring gifts of vegetables and animals to the islanders, so they would have new foods to eat.

Cook slowly sailed around New Zealand and found that it was two large islands. The channel between the islands is called Cook Strait today. Cook discovered that New Zealand was not part of a continent. After charting it, he sailed toward Australia. From there, he expected to continue on to England.

On to Australia

Only sections of Australia had been sighted by earlier explorers. Its true size was still unknown. Using his charting skills, Cook sailed up the eastern coast. This side of Australia was completely uncharted.

Cook soon learned that the land was large enough to be called a continent. It was not big enough to be the great Southern Continent, however.

Cook called one of the landing sites "Botany Bay" because of the great number of **exotic** plants and flowers found there. In the future, this bay would be the site of the first landing of English colonists.

By June 1770 Cook had almost completed his charts of the east coast. Then he and his crew suddenly had an accident that strongly tested Cook's skill.

The Coral Crash

"The ship struck and stuck fast," wrote Cook. The *Endeavour* had been coasting above the jagged **coral** of the gigantic 1,200-mile-long Great Barrier Reef. It seemed like a chore the crew could handle easily enough—until this surprise came.

Their wooden ship crashed and got caught on the underwater coral of the rough **reef.** The colorful coral was hard and very sharp.

The coral cut into the *Endeavour* and opened its hull to the sea. Water rushed in, flooding the ship. The nearest land was almost 25 miles away.

Cook and his crew showed courage and control. The wind was light, the moon was bright, the tide was high and the ship was stuck. Calmly, Cook gave orders to his crew. Calmly and swiftly, they obeyed.

First, they tried to pull the ship off the rock.

Throwing anchors to the sea, they tried to heave the anchor ropes wrapped around the **capstan.** The coral continued to grip the *Endeavour*.

Cook ordered almost everything thrown overboard to lighten the ship. Cannons, old food barrels, iron scrap—more than 40 tons in all—were taken out of the *Endeavour*. Still the coral held fast.

All four of the ship's pumps were set up to drain the seawater out of the hull. One of the pumps failed. Everyone on board took turns operating the other three pumps. They could barely keep the water from rising even higher inside the ship.

Only when the tide rose again the following evening did the *Endeavour* finally come loose. Now free in the water, the ocean was likely to fill the hull even faster. A sailor quickly measured its inside depth and found it had risen a foot and a half! The crew worked the pumps again and again.

Were they doomed to drown? The *Endeavour* was all alone, thousands of miles from home. Its few boats on deck could not save everyone.

Luck was with them. A large chunk of the coral stayed stuck in the hull, keeping much of the ocean outside. The sailor had measured from the wrong mark in the ship. The water was not rising so quickly, after all. The crew was glad to hear this news.

"It acted upon every man like a charm," Cook wrote; "they redoubled their vigor. . . . Before eight o'clock in the morning they gained considerably upon the leak."

Safe on Shore

Cook ordered the crew to seek a safe shore to beach and fix the ship. After two days' sailing, they found such a place. Today it is called Cook Harbor. While there Cook and his crew caught their first sight of kangaroos.

As soon as the ship was seaworthy, Cook set sail again. He and his crew continued along the eastern and northern coasts of Australia. Sometimes they sailed within inches of the great reef and its tall towering waves. Cook was the first one to have the courage to chart these coasts.

Continuing westward around the world by the charted oceans surrounding Asia and Africa, Cook and his crew returned to England in July 1771. Cook saw the king and was given the title of commander.

Cook's first around-the-world voyage was considered so successful that he was asked to command a second one. On this voyage, Commander Cook would sail as far south as possible to seek the Southern Continent.

THE SECOND VOYAGE

Antarctic Circle

The second voyage, starting in 1772, took Cook eastward all around cold and icy Antarctica. For extra safety, he sailed with two ships this time—the *Adventure* and the *Resolution*. Going farther south than the Antarctic Circle, Cook proved once and for all that there was no great Southern Continent in the warm zones of the Pacific Ocean. It was only a fantasy of earlier geographers and explorers.

In the Antarctic waters, Cook and his crew saw large numbers of whales, seals, penguins and other animals. Sometimes they almost collided with icebergs. The tops of some of the giant icebergs rose 200 feet above ocean level.

Cook tried to go as far south as he could. In his

journal he said that he wanted to go "not only farther than any other man before me, but as far as I think it possible for man to go."

Cook could not reach Antarctica, the ice-covered continent almost the size of two Australias. His ships were always blocked by ice. He thought the continent was there, however, since the ice was made from fresh-water snows that could only have formed on land.

Other Islands

Sailing across the Pacific, Cook came upon several other islands besides Tahiti and New Zealand. One of them was Easter Island, a land of giant stone statues. Another was Norfolk Island, a land of tall trees more than 100 feet high. Other islands included the Society Islands, the Tonga Islands, the New Hebrides, and New Caledonia.

Cook came back to England in July 1775. In honor of his efforts, he was given a new title. He was now called Captain Cook.

◆◆◆◆◆◆◆◆◆◆◆◆◆◆

CAPTAIN COOK'S NEXT VOYAGE

Captain Cook had now charted much of the South Pacific and shown that a warm Southern Continent did not exist. There was still one big question about the earth to answer. Was there a Northwest Passage—a northern waterway that connected the Atlantic Ocean to the Pacific? Such a passage could shortcut the long trip around Cape Horn.

Again Cook took two ships, the *Resolution* and the *Discovery,* to find the answer. Cook set sail from England in July 1776.

Sailing eastward around Africa and Australia, Captain Cook reached Tahiti in 1777. From there he crossed the equator just before Christmas.

Cook entered the North Pacific for the first

time. As the South Pacific had been before he came, the North Pacific was mostly uncharted. He named the first island he saw at this time Christmas Island.

In January 1778 Captain Cook came to two western members of the Hawaiian Islands—Niihau and Kauai. They did not appear on any charts. Landing at Kauai, Cook stayed only a couple of weeks and then sailed on to North America.

On to Alaska

After sighting land off the coasts of what are now Oregon and Washington, Cook continued up the coast of Canada. He kept looking for a wide waterway that would lead to the other side of the North American continent. After trading with Nootka Indians at Nootka Sound on what would later be called Vancouver Island, Captain Cook sailed on to Alaska and explored Cook Inlet.

In the summer of 1778 Cook came to the shortest width of the Bering Strait between Alaska and Asia. He crossed the Arctic Circle to 70 degrees latitude at a place he called Icy Cape.

After trying again and again, Cook could not find any openings in the Arctic Ocean ice. As winter came closer, he decided to return to the warm Hawaiian Islands to start fresh again the next year.

Hawaii Again

Captain Cook landed at Hawaii, the largest of the Hawaiian Islands, in January 1779. There, Captain Cook was treated like a god. The islanders thought Cook was their god Lono. He was given honors at their ceremonies and great feasts of food.

Cook set sail again in February. After a few days at sea, strong winds split the front mast of Cook's ship. Cook came back to Hawaii to repair it.

Some islanders were surprised at this early return. They had given all the gifts and food they could spare already. Trouble soon started. The islanders stole things from Cook that were important to him. When they took away one of his best boats, Cook felt they had gone too far. Cook needed this boat for close-in charting.

Cook's Conflict

Captain Cook went ashore with several men. They walked to the home of one of the top island chiefs. Cook asked the chief to come to his ship. Captain Cook thought he would keep the chief there until the boat was given back.

Cook got the chief to walk to the shore. A large crowd of islanders gathered at the site. They were ready and willing to fight to protect their chief.

The crowd did not want their chief to leave. They armed themselves with spears, stones, clubs and knives.

One islander came at Captain Cook with a knife. Since he did not wish to kill anyone, Cook fired a shot of small pellets onto the mat the islander wore over his chest. Cook hoped the loud sound would scare the islanders away.

Instead, when they saw the man was not killed, the islanders attacked in great numbers. Captain Cook and his men were caught by surprise.

"Take to the boats!" Captain Cook shouted. The men raced into the water. Their two landing boats floated in the ocean, within easy swimming distance.

If Cook could swim to the boats like the others, he would have a chance to escape. Although Cook had so many sailing skills, he seemed to have one clear weakness. Captain Cook, who had sailed across the great oceans of the world several times, may have never learned to swim.

Captain Cook was outnumbered by more than 100 to one. Within seconds, several islanders struck him with clubs and knives.

It happened quickly. Cook's crew shot their guns and cannons, but they were too late. Captain Cook and four of his men, the only ones still left on shore, were already killed.

The day was February 14, 1779. After the islanders saw that Captain Cook was dead and their chief was safe, they felt sorry for their actions. They tried to make peace with Cook's officers and crew.

The officers and crew buried the remains of Captain Cook in a ceremony at sea. One of the sad sailors said the crew felt like they had lost their father.

The officers continued Cook's voyage. Once more they looked for an ocean passage through North America. After many unsuccessful efforts they sailed home to England.

COOK'S EFFORTS INSPIRE OTHERS

Soon other explorers followed Cook's charts. Some tried to follow Cook's ideals too.

Cook was the first person to lead ships on scientific expeditions. Thousands of charts, drawings and descriptions of the lands and lives that Cook found were completed on his voyages. He was one of the first commanders to treat people of other lands, as well as his crew, in a kind and fair manner. Thanks to Cook's care, his voyages were the first to conquer scurvy. Cook also cleared up some of the last legends of geography. Actual knowledge of the world replaced an understanding based on old tales and fantasies.

Cook started a new age of scientific exploration. For the first time gaining knowledge became the main goal of future explorers. Like other great explorers, Captain Cook opened the minds of others to a wider world.

GLOSSARY

astronomy—The science of the stars, planets and other heavenly bodies.

capstan—A device for winding cables or ropes.

coral—Stony skeleton left by sea creatures.

crossbar—Also called a yard, it is a rod fastened across a ship's mast to support a sail.

exotic—Strikingly different or unusual.

equator—The imaginary circle around the middle of the earth halfway between the North and South poles.

expedition—A journey undertaken for scientific purposes.

geographers—Scientists who study the earth's surface.

latitude—The distance north or south from the equator.

longitude—The distance east or west from an imaginary standard line through Greenwich, England.

mast—A tall pole used to support a ship's sails and yards (crossbars).

mathematics—The science of numbers, forms and sizes.

navigation—The science of finding locations and plotting the course of ships.

reef—A coral or rock ridge close to the water's surface.

scurvy—A disease caused by lack of vitamin C, that is characterized by spongy gums, weakness, swelling and sores.

INDEX